NORMAN and the Bully

By Heather Young

Illustrations by Ramir Quintana

Edited by: Lisa Tabachnick

Heather Young, an Ottawa real estate agent, was born and raised in Ottawa, Ontario where she first developed her love of horses at the age of 4 and has continued that love affair throughout her life. Her first book "Norman", published in December 2012, won first place at both the Hollywood Book Festival and the Great Midwest Book Festival in the children's book category.

Norman, formerly known as Alydeed's Leader, is an ex-racehorse who is a descendant of Canadian racing royalty: Alydeed, 1992 Queen's Plate winner; and Northern Dancer, 1964 Kentucky Derby winner.

After his racing career Norman was surrendered to a horse rescue in Cameron, Ontario where he was adopted by Heather Young in 2010.

In the summer of 2011 Norman suffered an infection which ultimately cost him his right eye. Norman being the fighter he is and Heather's decision not to give up on him has given Norman a new lease on life, he is now enjoying his training as a hunter over fences and all the media attention he has attracted over the past year.

To order additional copies of this book, contact:
Xlibris LLC
1-888-795-4274
www.Xlibris.com
Orders@Xlibris.com

DEDICATION

Norman, who constantly overcomes every obstacle life throws at him.

Anyone who has ever been bullied and for all those who have stood up to a bully for a friend.

<u>Message from Norman:</u> Kids, Norman wants to let you know that if you're being bullied you should seek out a teacher, parent or trusted adult to help you.

$2.00 of every book sold will go to support
anti-bullying organizations

FOLLOW NORMAN:

NormanTheBook.webs.com
www.facebook.com/NormanTheHorse
https://twitter.com/NormanTheHorse

The last time we met Norman and his favourite rider Prudence, they were experiencing a terrific show jumping season, winning many competitions and impressing everyone around them. Norman had an amazing time but, truth be told, he was very happy to be back at the farm relaxing and playing with his friends.

One sunny afternoon at the farm, a few weeks after show season ended, a large truck pulling a horse trailer turned onto the farm driveway. All of the horses in the field, including Norman, stopped what they were doing and chased the trailer along the fence line to the parking lot in order to see the new horse.

As the trailer came to a stop near the barn, the ramp lowered and off walked a beautiful grey horse. His coat shone like a thunder cloud and his mane glistened like liquid silver. As he pranced down the ramp, Norman recognized him as the famed show jumping horse, Brutus, and was impressed that such a fine horse was going to be living at his farm.

Farmer Sue welcomed Brutus and took him inside the barn to show him his stall, which happened to be right next to Norman. When Norman came into his stall for dinner he was so excited to have a new neighbour that he immediately went to the shared wall to say hello. But, after using his loudest "knicker", Brutus didn't respond.

The next day Brutus noticed a news van in the parking lot. Being a famous show jumper, Brutus was used to the attention of reporters. As the news crew and Prudence came closer, Brutus flipped his long, flowing mane so he would look his best on film but they simply pushed past him and walked directly to Norman. Brutus was embarrassed to be ignored and decided he had to teach Norman a lesson for stealing his attention.

After the interview was done, Norman found the other horses, including Brutus, playing his favourite game of tag. As he approached the group to join in on the fun, Brutus pinned back his ears and showed Norman his teeth then gave Norman a hard bite right on his bottom. With that, Norman walked away sadly; he didn't understand why Brutus was being such a bully, after all he only wanted to be friends.

The following Thursday, Norman was getting a good bath and brushing so that he would be ready for a big horse show the next day. As Prudence finished brushing Norman and making sure he looked his very best, Brutus overheard her tell Norman to make sure he kept clean and to stay out of the mud.

Outside Norman was so careful to avoid walking through the puddles and stayed far away from his favourite place to roll in order to stay clean. However Brutus, remembering how Norman had stolen the spotlight from him, had other plans. As Norman had his head down drinking water, Brutus snuck up beside him carrying a rake in his mouth and quietly laid it down right next to Norman.

Brutus waited for the just right time and then made a loud noise which startled Norman. Norman reared up and, because he didn't see the rake, tripped and fell right into the huge mud puddle that he had tried so hard to avoid. As Norman looked up from the puddle, completely covered in mud, he saw Brutus trotting away, tail in the air and whinnying loudly.

That next morning when Prudence arrived to "trailer" Norman to the big show, she opened his stall door only to find the filthiest horse she had ever seen waiting to greet her. Though she was disappointed, Prudence couldn't help but laugh at the big bay horse covered head to toe in mud with his sad brown eyes staring back at her.

Prudence, laughing to herself, grabbed a horse brush and tried her best to clean Norman off before loading him onto the trailer. Brutus, listening from around the corner, couldn't help but be angry and disappointed that Norman didn't get into the trouble he thought he would for not staying clean.

That night Norman overheard Farmer Sue talking with Prudence. She told her how, after years of competing together, Brutus' rider decided he was now too old and replaced him with a younger horse. Norman realized why Brutus was being such a bully, he was sad. Norman understood how he felt because the thought of being replaced by Prudence had been one of his biggest fears after losing the sight in his right eye the year before.

That very next lesson day Norman put a plan into action. He waited for Prudence to see him, began limping and holding up his back leg pretending he was in pain. Concerned, Prudence checked Norman carefully and couldn't find anything wrong but, yet, he was still limping. Being cautious she asked Farmer Sue to keep an eye on Norman. As she looked around the field to see what other horse she could ride, she realized the only horse left was Brutus.

Prudence brought Brutus into the barn and started grooming him for their ride. As she was brushing Brutus, he remembered how nice it was to have someone make a fuss over him and how good it felt to be groomed. For the first time in a long time Brutus felt like himself again and that he still mattered.

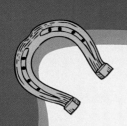

When Brutus and Prudence entered the riding arena everyone stopped to look, shocked to see Prudence riding a horse other than Norman. But, the crowd was also excited to see Brutus in action as they had heard about his famous show jumping past. Prudence and Brutus approached their first jump, Norman watched from the field as Brutus leaped gracefully into the air and landed on the other side.

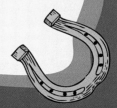

As Brutus looked back at the jump and at Prudence, he couldn't help but feel proud and happy. Out of the corner of his eye he spotted Norman who was standing on his hind legs doing a little dance. Brutus realized then that Norman had only pretended to be injured so that Prudence would choose him instead for the lesson. Knowing Norman had helped him, even after all the bad things he had done, made Brutus feel very ashamed of his actions.

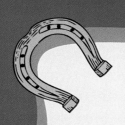

After Prudence removed his saddle and gave him a quick brushing, she led Brutus back into the paddock. But, before letting him go she gave him a large orange carrot as a reward for being so good during their ride. As she closed the gate, Prudence saw Brutus take the carrot in his mouth and drop it right in front of Norman. Norman, touched by the gesture, gently nuzzled Brutus' nose showing him there were no hard feelings.

Today Brutus has become one of the most popular horses on the farm. He now looks forward to Saturday when the cars drive up the laneway carrying riders to their lessons. He races along the fence line and waits to see his very own little rider, a young boy named Kevin, hop out of the car carrying a lovely red apple just for him.

Norman and Brutus have become the very best of friends, enjoying long runs through the tall grass and adventurous games of tag with the rest of the horses. When they compete against one another at horse shows, they are always cheering for each other.

You see, sometimes bullies don't mean to be bullies; it may be that someone (or some horse!) has simply forgotten what it's like to be loved and needs a friend to remind them they are special.

Edwards Brothers Malloy
Thorofare, NJ USA
February 17, 2014